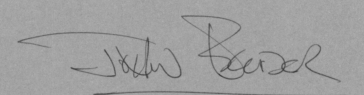

LOST PLACES
AND FORGOTTEN WORDS

COLORADO

JOHN FIELDER

FOREWORD BY RICHARD D. LAMM
PREFACE BY TIMOTHY E. WIRTH

WESTCLIFFE PUBLISHERS, INC. ENGLEWOOD, COLORADO

CONTENTS

International Standard Book Number: ISBN 0-942394-88-7
Library of Congress Catalogue Card Number: 88-51246
Copyright, Photographs and Text: John Fielder, 1989.
    All rights reserved.
Editor: John Fielder
Assistant Editor: Margaret Terrell Morse
Production Manager: Mary Jo Lawrence
Typographers: Richard M. Kohen and Dianne J. Borneman
Printed in Japan by Dai Nippon Printing Company, Ltd., Tokyo
Published by Westcliffe Publishers, Inc.,
    2650 South Zuni Street, Englewood, Colorado 80110

Bibliography

Beston, Henry. "The Outermost House." In *Especially Maine*. Brattleboro, Vt.: The Stephen Greene Press, 1976. Reprinted by permission.

Borland, Hal. *High, Wide and Lonesome*. Copyright © 1956 by Hal Borland. Copyright © 1984 by Barbara Dodge Borland. Used by permission of Frances Collin, literary agent.

*Bowles, Samuel. *The Switzerland of America*. Springfield, Mass.: S. Bowles, 1869.

Burland, Cottie. *Mythology of the Americas*. New York: The Hamlyn Publishing Group, 1970.

Dusenbery, Harris. "Ski the High Trail." 10th Mountain Division Collection, Western History Department, Denver Public Library.

*Faithfull, Emily. *Three Visits to America*. New York: Fowler & Wells, 1884.

*Grey, Zane. *Tales of Lonely Trails*. New York: Blue Ribbon Books, 1922. Reprinted by permission.

*Jackson, Helen Hunt. *Bits of Travel at Home*. Boston: Roberts, 1878.

Lavender, David. *The Rockies*. New York: Harper & Row, Publishers, 1968. Reprinted by permission of the author.

Lawrence, D.H. *Mornings in Mexico*. London: Secker, 1927.

Muir, John A.: from *A 1,000 Mile Walk to The Gulf*. Copyright 1916 by Houghton Mifflin Company. Copyright renewed 1944 by Ellen Muir Funk. Reprinted by permission of Houghton Mifflin Company.

*Parkman, Francis. *The Oregon Trail*.

*Roosevelt, Theodore. *Outdoor Pastimes of an American Hunter*. New York: Charles Scribner & Sons, 1908. Reprinted by permission.

*Stegner, Wallace. *This is Dinosaur*. New York: Alfred A. Knopf, Inc., 1983. Reprinted with permission.

Udall, Stewart L. *The Quiet Crisis and the Next Generation*. Layton, Utah: Gibbs Smith, 1988.

*Whitman, Walt. *Prose Works, Complete 1892*. Philadelphia: David McKay, 1897.

All selections preceded by * are found in *Chronicles of Colorado*, Frederick R. Rinehart, ed. Boulder, Colo.: Roberts Rinehart, Inc. Publishers, 1984.

Quotations located on opening pages of chapters are cited from *Mythology of the Americas*.

First Frontispiece: Morning skies reflect off the surface of Archuleta Lake, an alpine tarn resting high in the eastern end of the Weminuche Wilderness Area, San Juan Mountains.

Second Frontispiece: Alpine greens of July decorate mountain slopes below the spectacle of the Castles — eroded peaks in the West Elk Wilderness Area — a view from Storm Pass.

Title Page: Evening light bathes Anasazi dwellings in shades of orange. A Native American ruin more than 500 years old, Cutthroat Castle lies in a deserted canyon of southwestern Colorado's Hovenweep National Monument.

Right: Crusty March snows reflect the glow of morning light from Gothic Mountain in Gunnison National Forest.

RICHARD D. LAMM

FOREWORD

The philosopher Spinoza used to hide sugar cookies during the day in his papers so that, in the midst of his deep thoughts late at night, he would suddenly and unexpectedly come across a sugar cookie. What joy! What relief from the tedium of his work. Unexpected pleasure is always twice blessed. Colorado's joy is that it has so many natural equivalents of sugar cookies. Our "lost places" are, to me, our best places.

Every state has natural beauty, but it has clearly not been evenly distributed. Colorado, providentially, has gotten more than its share.

I fell in love with Colorado when I discovered her lost places. Stationed here in the Army in 1957, I used all my spare time to indulge my penchant for the outdoors. It was on these sojourns that I saw the scope and variety of Colorado. I found her hidden valleys and abandoned ghost towns. I kayaked the Dolores River, discovering hidden glens, grottoes and blind canyons. I rafted the Green and the Yampa. I hunted in North Park and sat in duck blinds in Lamar and in Weld County. I have climbed most of Colorado's 14,000-foot mountains and have seen the incredible lost places of the back country. I have cross-country skied from Crested Butte to Aspen and have seen how these lost places look in the snow.

Then, in my 39th year, I decided to walk the state as a way of getting around some of the awesome expense of campaigning. At three miles per hour, the world looks very different. Many things are opened up to you. Walking the state, watching the trees change, I again came across many of the unexpected pleasures that make up this great state.

What do these lost places mean? I would submit that there must be lost places for mankind to keep its sanity. They are clearly part of the geography of hope for our increasingly urbanized people. We must have ways to get away from the stink and pollution of our fellow man — for renewal, for rejuvenation and for worship.

The true goal of Colorado public policy cannot be to see how many people we can cram in with their automobiles and how much of our great state we can pave over; Colorado also must be concerned about and honor its lost places. It is important for us all to know that these places exist, that they are out there as an escape valve as we add people and economic growth to our fragile state.

There are many yardsticks to this civilization. One of them is economic growth. This may tell us how rich we are, but it doesn't tell us what kind of people we are. I would suggest that one of the defining factors that goes to the heart of what is truly Colorado is how many of these lost places we can keep to excite and inspire the next generation.

— RICHARD D. LAMM
Governor of Colorado, 1975–1987

In the warmth of storm-filtered light, Indian paintbrush wildflowers redden a verdant landscape high in the San Juan Mountains. In the background looms the bright face of Mount Hope, Weminuche Wilderness Area.

TIM WIRTH

PREFACE

When I first had the opportunity to leaf through a mock-up of this book, I opened the manuscript at random to a photograph of the Pawnee Buttes. Gazing at the picture, I had a sudden flash — *I've been there.* Turning the page I discovered another déjà vu image, of the Dolores River. The next few illustrations were not familiar, but toward the back I found a few more that were: The West Elk Wilderness Area — *I've ridden beneath those cliffs.* The Arikaree River on the Great Plains near Wray — *I've seen that from the air.* The Eagles Nest Wilderness Area — *I've climbed that peak.*

What most intrigues me about these coincidences is that John Fielder and I had never met until a few months ago. Yet somehow, without any prearrangement or discussion, we had been tracing and retracing each other's footsteps for a very long time. In different seasons in different years we had managed to reach many of the same destinations, to gaze on many of the same sights. But these uncanny parallels extend even further to encompass striking similarities in the evolution of our careers.

For 15 years both John Fielder and I have been doing our best to represent the great state of Colorado, he through photography, and I through politics. In 1974, the year I was first elected to Congress, John began taking the photographs that would be featured in *Colorado's Hidden Valleys*, his first book. In 1986, the year I ran for the Senate, John had just finished his second book, *Colorado, Images of the Alpine Landscape.* During the past five years, both of us have widened our horizons to include the far corners of the state. Now, finally, our paths have reached a welcome conflux here, in these pages.

Why have our journeys followed such congruent paths? To my mind, the only logical explanation is that we must share a powerful kinship. It's a kinship born of a shared love for Colorado's beauty, of a shared belief that protecting our state's unspoiled grandeur is of preeminent importance, of a shared conviction that "lost places" and "forgotten words" *matter.*

John tells me he's driven 60,000 miles and hiked another 1,200, ferreting out the exquisite photographs reproduced between these covers. Although I haven't kept track, I've probably traveled an equal distance meeting voters on the campaign trail and exploring proposed wilderness areas. Between us we've probably used every form of locomotion yet invented, including: helicopter, plane, Jeep, snowmobile, skis, snowshoes, mountain bike, raft, kayak, horse and llama. The upshot of all this wayfaring is that when it came time to select an image to grace this book's cover, John chose — by pure happenstance — a photograph of White Rock Mountain, a peak that lies a scant nine miles from the sagging Victorian house in Crested Butte that has long been a

weekend retreat for my wife, Wren, and our family.

In the living room of that house Wren keeps a cardboard box stuffed full of U.S. Geological Survey maps; she calls it her "topo box." One of the most creased and weather-beaten maps in the topo box is the "Gothic" quad, on which White Rock Mountain can be found near the headwaters of Copper Creek. Wren and I have hiked Copper Creek numerous times — and yet we've never seen White Rock look as glorious as it does on the cover of this book. That, of course, is John Fielder's special talent — the ability to capture fresh images, stirring photographs of peaks and valleys, of landscapes we may have glimpsed but most likely have never really *seen.*

It's the lucky senator who is privileged to represent Colorado in the U.S. Congress. Not only does Colorado possess an uncommonly independent and intelligent electorate, it is also one of the most beautiful states in the Union. Certainly, I would find the incessant back-and-forth travel the job demands nearly intolerable if I were not returning home each weekend to a cherished landscape. In this vein, it's interesting to note that Colorado congressmen, in striking contrast to politicians from other states, invariably return to Colorado when their tour of duty in Washington is up. The reason is clear: they have a place to come to. But why does Colorado summon such loyalty? What makes this state unique?

The flip — and erroneous — answer would be: the mountains. As every schoolchild learns, Colorado is the highest state in the nation, a point that perhaps can be best illustrated by observing that the *lowest* point in Colorado (3,350 feet, where the Arkansas River enters Kansas near the town of Holly) is higher than the *highest* point of 22 other states. Between Holly and the 14,433-foot top of Mount Elbert, Colorado's highest peak, lie more than 11,000 feet — two miles! — of vertical relief. Like many Westerners, I equate space with freedom; all that elbow room is a most welcome relief from the stifling congestion of the East.

Since I was a small boy I have enjoyed a heady romance with the Rockies, these towering alpine summits flung like a net across the sky. At some point during their lives, I'd encourage all Coloradans to visit Rocky Mountain National Park, Pikes Peak, Longs Peak, the Maroon Bells and the rest of our state's "crown jewels." But although the Rockies are truly spectacular, they are not what makes Colorado unique.

According to geographers, what gives our state its singular status is that it encompasses parts of three physiographic provinces: the Great Plains, the Rockies and the Colorado Plateau. Unfortunately, in both a literal and a figurative sense, the majestic Rockies too frequently overshadow the sprawling plains to the east and the canyon country to the

---

Sandstone canyons of southeastern Colorado activate thoughts of southern Utah. The Purgatoire River dissects the plains of southeastern Colorado on its journey between the towns of Trinidad and Las Animas.

west. This is perfectly understandable — but a shame nonetheless. What excites me about this book is that John has selected images from the *entire* state, in effect reclaiming those parts of Colorado that so often get short shrift.

When it hasn't simply been ignored, the eastern third of Colorado has been much maligned. Contrary to rumor, this is not some monotonous blizzard-prone wasteland. Eastern Colorado is part of the aptly named Great Plains. The plains, of course, are famous for their vast vistas. Walking across them I sometimes feel as though I can sense the entire sweep of history; visions of dinosaurs and mammoths, Indians hunting buffalo, and settlers struggling with their wagons race through my consciousness. Today, amid farms and ranches, one can find more than a few "lost places" inlaid into this prairie, like turquoise in a ring.

Last year I had an opportunity to visit one of these hidden gems, the Purgatory River canyon east of Walsenburg. I was astounded to discover that along part of its course the Purgatory has cut a sandstone canyon nearly 1,000 feet deep. This canyon — John has a picture of it in this book — is simply stunning, the more so because its presence comes as such a sweet surprise.

West of the Continental Divide our state is as rough as a washboard. Here you find a tortured topography shot full of nooks and crannies, a place where canyons, mesas, mountains and badlands are jumbled together in what amounts to a physiographic slumgullion. Historically, this rich stew has nourished Indians, hunters, geologists, ranchers, biologists, photographers, outlaws, backpackers — just about anybody who delights in the unexpected and doesn't mind scrabbling to get by.

In the last few years, thanks largely to the generosity of an assortment of somewhat-nefarious boatmen (rowdy and disheveled, they are best left unnamed), Wren and I have discovered that the Western Slope is a storehouse of "lost places." Running the whitewater rapids of the Gunnison, Dolores and Green rivers has been a wonderful experience. Each of these canyons — and others we have explored on horseback and on foot — is a kaleidoscopic visual feast, presenting new sights around each bend. As you float past a side canyon, choked with cottonwoods and blocked by a dry waterfall, the hauntingly sweet trill of a canyon wren descends. Such moments reek of the "lost place" aura that John has so vividly captured in his photographs.

John Fielder's images feed that part of me that hungers for and is refreshed by natural beauty. Whenever I weary of politicking and the campaign trail, I recharge my batteries by traipsing around Colorado's outback for a few days. These sojourns have a value for me that far surpasses their short duration. Hearing an elk bugling, feeling the pull of a cutthroat trout on my line, rafting an unbridled river, observing the splendor of a late summer sunset — experiences like these reaffirm my belief in the value of wild places and the importance of protecting them.

Although most of Colorado's crown jewels were saved long ago, in recent years legislation I have introduced to protect 12 wilderness areas (including some depicted in these pages) has been at a standstill. The fate of 700,000 acres has been held hostage by partisan bickering between developers and environmentalists. This is unfortunate. Wilderness areas meet a host of human needs — recreation, quiet, natural beauty, spiritual inspiration. Preservation of our natural resources isn't simply good environmental policy; it's also good economic policy. Recreation and tourism are now Colorado's second largest industry. In 1985, tourists spent $4 billion in Colorado, generating 103,000 jobs and $550 million in total tax revenues. The fact is, wilderness pays. We need more of it. It's time to move forward to safeguard Colorado's remaining "lost places," the fast-vanishing remnants of our state's pristine beauty.

By his inspired pairing of "forgotten words" with images of "lost places," John Fielder reminds us that our natural heritage and cultural heritage are inextricably intertwined — and that we cannot save one without saving the other. Wilderness is part of our history; history is part of our wilderness. Both are invaluable birthrights, inseparable touchstones. Yet I sometimes worry that the onrushing future threatens to cleave Coloradans from our past.

Colorado has always been a meeting ground, a rendezvous region, a boom-and-bust place where people came, mingled and — most often — left. My ancestors were some of those who stayed. As a fourth-generation Coloradan I believe those of us who are "stickers" (to use historian Wallace Stegner's term) must cling like burrs to our remembrances. It's our duty to ensure that Colorado history is not consigned to a dusty museum somewhere. Like a trail above treeline marked with cairns, our history is full of dates and developments and lessons that together represent the only trustworthy guide we have to an uncertain future.

Some people might argue that it makes no difference if lost places stay lost and forgotten words stay forgotten. I disagree. To my mind, lost places and forgotten words can be thought of as trailheads, departure points for cultivating a deeper understanding of our state and its history, providing an opportunity to mount what the Spanish conquistadors called an "entrada," a personal journey of discovery.

John Fielder's photographs offer irrefutable proof that if we undertake that journey in the right frame of mind, there is no reason that a beaver pond in the Holy Cross Wilderness, say, cannot appear as fresh and unsullied to us as it did to a fur trapper 150 years ago. Or that the Book Cliffs near Grand Junction, as grey and wrinkled as an elephant skin, cannot delight us as they did Father Escalante, the Spanish priest who traveled there in 1776. Or that Echo Park, where looming cliffs overhang the confluence of the Green and Yampa rivers, cannot awe us as it did John Wesley Powell in 1869.

The take-home message of this book is that by preserving lost places and forgotten words for posterity, we can ensure that future generations will be able to experience the explorer's thrill at discovering something new. What better gift to leave our grandchildren?

As succeeding generations of Coloradans discover their rich heritage, they may learn a lesson my wanderings have taught me: Retracing the footsteps of those who went before is in no way an idle exercise. Now, more than ever, it pays to look around.

And this book is a good place to start.

— TIM WIRTH
U.S. Senator, Colorado

Over 13,000 feet in elevation, White Rock Mountain dominates the valley whose headwaters spill into Copper Creek drainage on the southern end of the Maroon Bells – Snowmass Wilderness Area. *Overleaf: Orange lichen and the warmth of rain-filtered light unite to paint stark cliffs of the Chinese Wall — from a ledge immediately below the vast plateau of the Flat Tops Wilderness Area.*

JOHN FIELDER

INTRODUCTION

Over the past four years, while making these photographs, I hiked many miles in search of nature's most glorious moments. What began as a quest to become acquainted with the sights, sounds and smells of "the rest" of Colorado ended with much more than just sensory stimulation and memories on film. The past four years ended with an "awakening" high upon cliffs in southwestern Colorado.

The Anasazi

It must have been that first view of Anasazi dwellings cemented into sheer sandstone walls that rekindled my passion for the land. Or maybe the absolute antiquity of these deserted 800-year-old ruins was the catalyst. I only know that something sent a shiver through me as my binoculars brought the doorstep of the Eagles Nest ruin to me. I was immediately self-conscious, and a feeling overcame me that I was spying. I felt a presence, as if I were not alone, as if the inhabitants had not truly departed this place.

I was awestruck by the idea that a significant civilization had once lived within the very canyons I was now exploring, and overwhelmed by the fact that I knew nothing about it. As I climbed high along steep ridges to visit these ancient ruins, scattered pottery sherds fueled the anxiety I felt "trespassing" on this people's land and the curiosity growing within me to know more about them.

A 20-foot climb up a rickety old ladder placed me on a narrow shelf in the middle of a 200-foot sandstone cliff. I was greeted by a path, no wider in some places than three feet, hugging the great rock wall. It followed the rocky ledge and connected me with the first of several disintegrating domiciles. Each was constructed of sandstone slabs, mortar and a few logs. The front wall of each building was flush with the edge of the cliff.

The next evening I was perched on the edge of a ruin in a different canyon, waiting for the declining sun to create a photograph for me. The quality of light I was hoping for never did occur, but I used the waiting time to contemplate the significance of my situation. Clearly a great society had once existed within the hundreds of canyons and thousands of ruins around Mesa Verde and the rest of what is now the Four Corners region of Colorado, New Mexico, Utah and Arizona. I was astonished that these people had chosen to settle in such an inhospitable place — great heat and cold, a paucity of water, a dearth of land suitable for crops, not to mention having to raise a family on a rocky ledge! What could possibly have motivated a people to live in this region since before the time of Christ?

The Culture of the Pueblo People

My curiosity about the *Anasazi* (a Navajo term meaning "ancient ones") led me to explore not only their culture as revealed to us by the science of archaeology, but also the culture of contemporary Native Americans, the tribes that are the descendants of the Anasazi. The Hopi tribe of northern Arizona and the Rio Grande Pueblo tribes of New Mexico are thought to be descended from the Mesa Verde Anasazi. The Zuni Puebloans of northwestern New Mexico are probably descended from the Mogollons, ancients whose culture resembled that of the Anasazi.

Though the mythology and religion of the ancient southwestern Native Americans varies from tribe to tribe, there are many similarities. Emotional attachment to the land they dwelled upon dominated their lives and religion. The homeland was the center of their universe, and no common forces of nature could impel them to leave. Severe drought is probably the reason that the Mesa Verde Anasazi permanently abandoned their cliff dwellings around the year 1250.

Today's Pueblo people live in the same rugged desert environment. They are there because it is their home, where their ancestors persevered 1,000 years before them, and they have always persistently resisted relocation by the U.S. government. Belief in their religion and an intimate knowledge of their heritage seem to have provided the Puebloans with the strength needed to endure and enjoy such a world.

These are a successful people who in early times sustained their culture much longer than the Incas and the Aztecs to the south. They lived with and survived Spanish culture for more than 200 years, and have also endured the stress of living with a constantly changing U.S. culture. Is there something for us non-Native Americans to learn by gaining a better understanding of Pueblo culture?

In *To the Inland Empire*, Stewart Udall, one of our country's great conservationists, says of the ancient Pueblo people:

> [They] were in constant communion with the natural world. Harmony was a central theme of their worship: they sought harmony with nature, harmony with other Indian groups, harmony with the members of their own villages. The social goals the Pueblos distilled out of centuries of living in a demanding environment were amity, not conquest; stability, not strife; conservation, not waste; restraint, not aggression.

In today's age of nuclear catastrophes, ocean oil spills, destruction of the ozone layer, and apathy for the degree to which we live in harmony with the natural world, a look back in time generates questions we should ask ourselves. Should we be paying more attention to the standards of the Anasazi and their descendants? Toward what end are we taking our civilization if we do not arrest our disrespect for the natural environment? Certainly it is not necessary to consult a Zuni Priest to gain that answer, though he might

---

Deep within the dunes, sunflowers add life to the sterility of a landscape dominated by wind-blown sands, Great Sand Dunes National Monument, San Luis Valley.

be able to help us mitigate the damage we've already done. To quote Udall from his book *The Quiet Crisis and the Next Generation*:

> It is ironical that today the conservation movement finds itself turning back to ancient Indian land ideas, to the Indian understanding that we are not outside of nature, but of it. From this wisdom we can learn how to conserve the best parts of our continent.

About This Book

As I poured over thousands of photographs in search of the right ones to put into this book, the inspiration and example of the Native Americans took hold of me. The images seemed to fall into categories that coincidentally followed and related to the Zuni story of the creation of the world. Though only parts of this story are printed at the beginning of each of the book's chapters, the essence of the myth provided me a wonderful way to segment the photographs.

Colorado is so much more than just the Rocky Mountains. Unfortunately, I have only recently discovered that fact. These past four years I have explored some of the most remote mountain wildernesses in our state and witnessed many exciting moments unique to any I experienced in the first decade of my career as a nature photographer. At the same time I discovered many new Colorado places that were unlike any I had seen before.

West of the Rockies lies the Colorado Plateau, through which flow a number of Colorado rivers on their way to the Pacific. Before they leave our state, the Colorado, Green, Yampa and Dolores rivers plunge precipitously through giant canyons. Water erosion has carved spectacular formations all over western Colorado, and the scenery is both breathtaking and infinite. East of the Rockies are high, semi-arid plains that appear to be quite flat, but in many places are clearly the opposite. Broad escarpments, high buttes, deep river canyons and ubiquitous spring wildflowers make this part of Colorado a joy to visit. From one side of the state to the other, the sights, sounds and smells are as different from one another as the peace-loving Zunis were from the aggressive Spanish explorers who subjugated them in centuries past.

I call the locations depicted within this book "lost places," for they are either remote from civilization or simply not often visited by people. To accompany the photographs, I have included the words of a number of great writers who have experienced Colorado's natural world first hand or who simply possess an abiding love for our planet and its environment. Some of these people wrote their words long ago, others in recent times, but in each case the wisdom imparted in these "forgotten words" might be useful to those who seek to live in harmony with nature.

— JOHN FIELDER
Denver

For their encouragement and support, I dedicate this book to my mother and father.

The falling autumn sun highlights a snag against evening skies. West Spanish Peak lies behind, Spanish Peaks Wilderness Study Area, San Isabel National Forest.

Sky
Father...

"Before creation began there was only the 'one who contains everything', Awonawilona; otherwise there was blackness and nothingness. Awonawilona created life within himself; the mists of increasing and the streams of growing flowed from him. He assumed a form and was the maker of light, the sun. When the sun appeared the mists gathered together and fell as water, becoming the sea in which the world floats. From within himself Awonawilona formed seed and impregnated the waters. Then, in the warmth of the sun, green scum formed over the great waters and became solid and strong. It was divided and became Earth Mother of the Four Directions and Sky Father who covers everything."

In the Rocky Mountains, end of day is celebrated with pastel skies that this time bear no rain, Rawah Wilderness Area, Medicine Bow Mountains.   Above: On Colorado's northeastern high plains, end of day is made distinct by silhouettes of the Pawnee Buttes against vacant skies, Pawnee National Grasslands.

"...[We] looked into [the lakes'] waters, and on over them to the mountains, — first green, then blue, then black, finally white, and then higher to clouds, as changing in color under storm, under sun, under moon, under lightning. Every variety of scene, every change and combination of cloud and color were offered us in these two days; and we worshipped, as it were, at the very fountains of beauty, where its every element in nature lay around, before, and above us."   — Samuel Bowles, *The Switzerland of America*

The last vestiges of light reflect onto a tarn in the enormous Missouri Creek cirque. Mounts Belford and Oxford loom in the distance, Collegiate Peaks Wilderness Area.

"We watched the flare of the sunset and we looked out over the endless rolling plains. . . . I looked at the horizon to the east, but I couldn't see beyond the plains. In the eastern sky, maybe half as far away as Nebraska, was a long thin cloud all pink and lavender with reflected sunset. I wondered if they could see that cloud in Nebraska."

— Hal Borland, *High, Wide and Lonesome*

As so often occurs here, the evening sun makes fire in the sky above the high plains of northeastern Colorado — from the riverbed of the Arikaree River, Yuma County.

"The clouds opened at the point where they first had gathered, and the whole sublime congregation of mountains was bathed at once in warm sunshine. They seemed more like some vision of eastern romance than like a reality of that wilderness; all were melted together into a soft delicious blue, as voluptuous as the sky of Naples . . .

With dense clouds tacked closely to the horizon, it appeared that the sun would make no color this day. Yet it found a slit at the last possible moment, Eagles Nest Wilderness Area, Gore Range.

. . . or the transparent sea that washes the sunny cliffs of Capri. On the left the sky was still of an inky blackness; but two concentric rainbows stood in bright relief against it, while far in front the ragged clouds still streamed before the wind, and the retreating thunder muttered angrily."

— Francis Parkman, *The Oregon Trail*

Clouds shaped like rooster tails often portend the approach of bad weather. The rains came a day later in this case, Rawah Wilderness Area, Medicine Bow Mountains.

"We have now reach'd, penetrated the Rockies ... and though these chains spread away in every direction, specially north and south, thousands and thousands farther, I have seen specimens of the utmost of them, and know henceforth at least what they are, and what they look like. Not themselves alone, for they typify stretches and areas of half the globe — are, in fact, the vertebrae or back-bone of our hemisphere."

— Walt Whitman, *Prose Works* . . .

A small tarn reflects the beginning of afternoon showers, Willow Creek cirque, Maroon Bells – Snowmass Wilderness Area.

"Some days there would be clouds, big puffy clouds blue around the edges, and the clouds always made the sky a deeper blue. I would lie on my back and watch the clouds sail over and feel the biting chill when their shadows struck me. . . . And the cloud shadows weren't blue or purple as they had been all summer; now they were gray or black."

— Hal Borland, *High, Wide and Lonesome*

Low clouds part to reveal great thunderheads growing high above the plains of eastern Colorado, Washington County.

Sunrise on the edge of Ute Canyon,
Colorado National Monument.

" . . . the chasm, the gorge, the crystal mountain stream, repeated scores,
hundreds of miles — the broad handling and absolute uncrampedness —
the fantastic forms, bathed in transparent browns, faint reds and grays,
towering sometimes a thousand, sometimes two or three thousand feet
high — at their tops now and then huge masses pois'd, and mixing with
the clouds, with only their outlines, hazed in misty lilac, visible."

— Walt Whitman, *Prose Works . . .*

Whites and grays of afternoon cumulus clouds enhance the spectacle of the alpine environment where Rock Creek meanders
through lush meadows, Weminuche Wilderness Area.

Hues of predawn light provide a backdrop to 14,017-foot Wilson Peak. A nearly full moon sets behind its north ridge, Uncompahgre National Forest.

"But perhaps as I gaze around me the rarest sight of all is in atmospheric hues. The prairies — as I cross'd them in my journey hither — and these mountains and parks, seem to be to afford new lights and shades. Everywhere the aerial gradations and sky-effects inimitable; nowhere else such perspectives, such transparent lilacs and grays."

— Walt Whitman, *Prose Works . . .*

Pink rays of predawn light can be seen only by those who rise before the sun. This show of light occurred one hour before sunrise, Weminuche Pass, Weminuche Wilderness Area.

"On the day after, we had left the mountains at some distance. A black cloud descended upon them, and a tremendous explosion of thunder followed, reverberating among the precipices. In a few moments everything grew black, and the rain poured down like a cataract."
— Francis Parkman, *The Oregon Trail*

A lone cottonwood tree anticipates more spring showers that will replenish a transitory pasture pond, which will be dry in just a few weeks, along the East Fork Williams Fork River, northeastern Colorado.

"I had no conception of acreage or distance. To me, that whole expanse of hillside across the valley and the tableland beyond were ours. Father felt a kinship with the plains, but to me they were a personal possession. What are the boundaries of boyhood, anyway? That land, as far as I could see, belonged to me. The school section, with its great beds of cactus, were to become mine, and so were the flats off to the south, with their huge prairie dog town. So was the whole of Ketchem Holler, even John Gerrity's big sheep camp where the prickly poppies grew lush in summer and the doves haunted the empty sheds in winter. So were the sand hills still farther to the north. The boundaries of boyhood, as I knew them for a time, were that thin, distant line of the horizon; and even that did not bound the dreams and the imagination. Long later, when I first saw the red stone house where Daniel Boone was born in the red hills of Pennsylvania, I understood why he had to go and see far places. That red stone house was set in a cup of hills, every one a challenge. Those who live with a far horizon in their boyhood are never again bound to a narrow area of life. They may bind themselves, but that is a different matter."

— Hal Borland, *High, Wide and Lonesome*

From the middle of the Pawnee National Grasslands rise two buttes that can be seen from many miles away. Soft, chalky soils complement the pastels of morning light, Pawnee Buttes.

"Bound to suns and planets by invisible cords, I feel the flame of eternity in my soul. Here, in the midst of the every-day air, I sense the rush of ethereal rains. I am conscious of the splendour that binds all things of earth to all things of heaven. . . ." — Helen Keller, *My Religion*

Sunrise will soon cast light on a section of mountain tumbled from a high ridge, Sangre de Cristo Wilderness Study Area.

As sunset dims, 14,414-foot Mount Harvard is the last peak to receive its light, Collegiate Peaks Wilderness Area.

Morning May rains green
the environs of the Pawnee
National Grasslands.

Earth Mother...

"Earth and Sky lay in union and the fourfold womb of Earth conceived all creatures. Then she separated from Sky. She would not give birth yet; all must be prepared. So Earth and Sky assumed the forms of man and woman and discussed the creation of the earth. Earth Mother held a bowl of water and described how the mountains should be made to divide land from land, and stand around the rim of the world."

The hike up to Willow Pass is steep, but provides fine views of North Maroon Peak and Maroon Peak — the Maroon Bells. Red rock distinguishes the region, Maroon Bells – Snowmass Wilderness Area.   Above: Peaks of the Ruby Range catch morning light, one after the other, in order of their elevations. Waters beside Yule Creek mirror the event, Raggeds Wilderness Area.

"On one side was a steep hill of sage and aspens, and on the other a black, spear-pointed spruce forest, rising sheer to a bold, blunt peak patched with snow-banks, and bronze and gray in the clear light. Huge white clouds sailed aloft, making dark moving shadows along the great slopes." — Zane Grey, *Tales of Lonely Trails*

Aspen trees on the wrong side of Gothic Valley await morning light that has already provided warmth to Gothic Mountain, Gunnison National Forest.

"After sunset . . . gray shadows darkened and gloom penetrated the aisles of the forest, until all the sheltered places were black as pitch. The spruces looked spectral — and speaking. The silence of the woods was deep, profound, and primeval. It all worked on my imagination until I began to hear faint sounds, and finally grand orchestral crashings of melody."   — Zane Grey, *Tales of Lonely Trails*

White Rock Mountain basks in the light of the setting sun as high alpine ridges shade conifers across the valley. Copper Creek lies in between, Maroon Bells – Snowmass Wilderness Area.

Erratic boulders lie on ridges of the Needle Mountains. Eolus, Sunlight and Windom peaks surround this basin, which is home to two lakes and a herd of wild goats, Weminuche Wilderness Area.

White boulders turn blue under a clear morning sky. Their source rises high into the August sky, along the headwaters of Cataract Creek, Eagles Nest Wilderness Area, Gore Range.

"The universe is not hostile, nor yet is it friendly. It is simply indifferent."
— John Haynes Holmes, *The Sensible Man's View of Religion*

The poetic shapes of Wheeler Geologic Wilderness Study Area require no sun. The ubiquitous cracks and crevices outline years of constant erosion, San Juan Mountains.

A low-lying sun casts distinct shadows across the dunes. When the sun is high in the sky these lines are lost, and so, too, is the visual poetry of Great Sand Dunes National Monument.

"Talk, I say again, of going to Europe, of visiting the ruins of feudal castles, or Coliseum remains, or kings' palaces — when you can come *here*. The alternations one gets, too; after the Illinois and Kansas prairies of a thousand miles — smooth and easy areas of the corn and wheat of ten million democratic farms in the future — here start up in every conceivable presentation of shape, these non-utilitarian piles, coping the skies, emanating a beauty, terror, power, more than Dante or Angelo ever knew. Yes, I think the chyle of not only poetry and painting, but oratory, and even the metaphysics and music fit for the New World, before being finally assimilated, need first and feeding visits here."

— Walt Whitman, *Prose Works* . . .

Mushrooms 30 feet high dominate this horizon in southeastern Colorado. Eroded forms lend relief to the otherwise flat topography, Indian Paintpot Mines.

"Near one's eyes ranges an infinite variety; high up, the bare whitey-brown, above timber line; in certain spots afar patches of snow any time of year; (no trees, no flowers, no birds, at those chilling altitudes.) As I write I see the Snowy Range through the blue mist, beautiful and far off. I plainly see the patches of snow." — Walt Whitman, *Prose Works . . .*

Clouded afternoon light intensifies complementary reds and greens of the Maroon Bells – Snowmass Wilderness Area — a view from Frigid Air Pass, whose name aptly describes the conditions at the time.

The colors of Frigid Air Pass recur 4,000 feet below and a few hundred miles away in a side canyon of the Green River, Dinosaur National Monument, northwestern Colorado.

"The ancient values of dignity, beauty and poetry which sustain [human life] are of nature's inspiration; they are born of the mystery and beauty of the world. Do no dishonor to the earth lest you dishonor the spirit of man. Hold your hands out over the earth as over a flame. To all who love her, who open to her the doors of their veins . . .

A hike into the heart of the Book Cliffs reveals a landscape unique in Colorado. Perhaps taken for granted, this scenery near the city of Grand Junction is extraordinary.

. . . she gives of her strength, sustaining them with her own measureless tremor of dark life. Touch the earth, love the earth, honor the earth, her plains, her valleys, her hills and her seas; rest your spirit in her solitary places. For the gifts of life are the earth's and they are given to all. . . ."
— Henry Beston, *The Outermost House*

Ice and snow patterns on sand dunes are unusual, but not on the dunes at Great Sand Dunes National Monument, which rise above 8,000 feet and are the highest in North America.

" . . . the heights of the mountains and the depths of the canyons were
beyond the norm. One went about totally sensitized. . . . God was a pagan
god, in the air, over the mountains, in the waterfalls. But how can I give
the feeling-tone of my childhood in that high Alpine valley, which simply
is one of the most beautiful spots in the world?"

— Theodora Kroeber, Letter to David Lavender, *The Rockies*

Ancient glaciers are responsible for the carving of alpine valleys in the Weminuche Wilderness Area, San Juan Mountains.

Waters of the Yampa River race through Warm Springs Rapid in Dinosaur National Monument, northwestern Colorado.

In spring, waters will flow from snows deposited in the dead of winter at the high elevations, Collegiate Peaks Wilderness Area.

"The land and the Indians were bound together by the ties of kinship and nature, rather than by an understanding of property ownership. 'The land is our mother.' "   — Stewart Udall, *The Quiet Crisis and the Next Generation*

A cool October morning turns the cold water of a small lake into glass. Two Purple mountains and two Ruby ranges are better than one, on the edge of the Raggeds Wilderness Area.

" . . . the larger of the two rivers, the Green, is the longest fork of the
Colorado; and . . . it used to be called the Seedskeedee-Agie, the Prairie
Hen River, by the Crows, and by the Spaniards the Rio Verde. Its tributary
the Yampa is even yet by some people and some maps called the Bear."
— Wallace Stegner, *This is Dinosaur*

Steamboat Rock duplicates itself in still side waters of the Green River just one mile from the Green's rendezvous with the
Yampa River, Dinosaur National Monument.

"The last ice sheet to thrust south from the pole did not actually touch the American Rockies. Nevertheless, the chill that spread throughout the area was such that snow piled high on the ridges and then compacted into glaciers that scoured relentlessly as gravity dragged the ice down the slopes. Its gouging created deep, steep-walled cirques at timberline and above. Sometimes these cirques lie close together, separated only by thin aretes whose upper ends pull together in sky-scratching horn peaks, beloved by photographers." — David Lavender, *The Rockies*

Gilded with nature's gold by aspen trees and October light, Mount Sneffels has never appeared more regal, above North Dallas Creek, Uncompahgre National Forest.

Filtered by the vestiges of a transitory storm, the descending sun warms an aspen-covered flank of West Spanish Peak. Sierra Blanca Massif looms in the distance, Spanish Peaks Wilderness Study Area.

"... there passed nearly a thousand years after the last of the Fremont people departed during which, as far as history knows, these canyons were only wind and water and stone, space and sky and the slow sandpapering of erosion, the unheard scurry of lizard and scream of mountain lion, the unseen stiff-legged caution of deer, the unnoted roar of rapids in the dark slot of Lodore and the unrecorded blaze of canyon color darkening with rain and whitening with snow and glaring in the high sun of solstice."

— Wallace Stegner, *This is Dinosaur*

Precambrian rock of the Green River canyon absorbs the light of the ascending sun. This ancient red rock dominates the canyon, Dinosaur National Monument.

"Dawn came there on the ridge, at first just a faint lightening on the eastern horizon, a line of milky blue beneath the deep, deep blue embedded with stars. The milky blue spread upward, and lower stars in the east faded and vanished."   Hal Borland, *High, Wide and Lonesome*

In predawn light, fresh snow overlies the eroded shapes of the Indian Paintpot Mines. With a complete spectrum of colored soils, this may have been the source of ceremonial paints, eastern Colorado.

"A myth has grown up that the high country also influences the basic nature of the people who dwell in it — men to match the mountains, so to speak. The notion has certain superficials to recommend it. Altitude, dryness, and long successions of sunny days do produce an invigorating climate. Tremendous vistas, ever changing under each day's varying slant of light, do fascinate even those who are used to the scene."

— David Lavender, *The Rockies*

The spires that surround Twin Lakes Basin make this alpine cirque as impressive as any in Colorado, the headwaters of Needle Creek in the Needle Mountains, Weminuche Wilderness Area.

"Let children walk with Nature, let them see the beautiful blendings and communions of death and life, their joyous inseparable unity, . . . and they will learn that death is stingless indeed, and as beautiful as life, and that the grave has no victory, for it never fights."
— John Muir, *1,000 Mile Walk to the Gulf*

East Rim Arch was manufactured by water, not by wind, as were the arches of southern Utah, in Rattlesnake Canyon of the Black Ridge Wilderness Study Area, western Colorado.

Morning light reflected from canyon walls adds color to sandstone rocks. This draw descends into the Yampa River near Mantle Ranch, Dinosaur National Monument.

Rain from the Clouds...

"[Earth Mother] spat into the [bowl of] water and stirred it with her fingers making foam arise. She drew milk from her breasts to give it life. So she indicated the coming of life, and showed how children should be nourished. She breathed upon the foam, and mists and rainbows arose as clouds floating above the sea. The Sky breathed and rain fell from the clouds. This showed how man would find warmth and life near Earth Mother and cold from Sky Father, whose breath would bring fertilising rain to Earth again."

Serenity and *tranquility* are defined aptly by this image of spring-fed tarns at 12,300 feet. A more peaceful morning has never occurred, Ute Pass, Weminuche Wilderness Area. Above: Summer snowmelt cascades on its way into the North Fork of the Crystal River below Geneva Lake, Maroon Bells – Snowmass Wilderness Area.

"The colors of the rocks vary from a rich red-brown to vermilion, from gray to almost sugar-white, with many shades of pink and buff and salmon in between. The cliffs and sculptured forms are sometimes smooth, sometimes fantastically craggy, always massive, and they have a peculiar capacity to excite the imagination; the effect on the human spirit is neither numbing nor awesome, but warm and infinitely peaceful."

— Wallace Stegner, *This Is Dinosaur*

Waters of the Yampa River, canyon walls and the saturated light of the setting sun transform Dinosaur National Monument into another world, near Big Joe Rapid.

The West Branch of the Laramie River plunges through fog-enshrouded Roosevelt National Forest high in the Medicine Bow Mountains, Rawah Wilderness Area.

"The spiritual contrast and etheriality of the whole region consist largely to me in its never-absent peculiar streams — the snows of inaccessible upper areas melting and running down through the gorges continually. Nothing like the water of pastoral plains, or creeks with wooded banks and turf, or anything of the kind elsewhere."
— Walt Whitman, *Prose Works . . .*

Early snows envelop the landscape along the West Fork of Clear Creek, but warm temperatures will quickly consume all whiteness, Arapaho National Forest.

The North Fork of the Crystal River plummets out of Fravert Basin. Its leisurely descent is abruptly altered by cliffs of the Maroon Bells – Snowmass Wilderness Area.

"Contrary to what the song says, there is very little springtime in the Rockies. It is a dull, soggy, fitful time, melting icicles one hour and blowing snow the next. But the drifts do shrink, water pours down the hillsides, the bare branches of the quaking aspens mist with green. The sun rises earlier and ascends straight overhead. . . . Suddenly — more suddenly each year than you are prepared for — July arrives."

— David Lavender, *The Rockies*

The color green is well defined by sopping meadows brimming with fresh snowmelt under clear blue skies — looking down into Upper Slate Lake Basin, Eagles Nest Wilderness Area, Gore Range.

Fed by melting snows from a fierce winter, Slate Creek plunges toward a rendezvous with the Blue River, Eagles Nest Wilderness Area, Gore Range.

Native grasses and an unspoiled ecology portray the environs of the Arikaree River (and its sometimes meager waters) as they were a thousand years ago, northeastern Colorado.

Promontories of the Purgatoire River contradict the belief that eastern Colorado is flat. Morning light drenches sandstone in red, Piñon Canyon area, southeastern Colorado.

"There are, today, a few wilderness reaches on the North American continent — in Alaska, in Canada, and in the high places of the Rocky Mountains — where the early-morning mantle of primeval America can be seen in its pristine glory, where one can gaze with wonder on the land as it was when the Indians first came. Geologically and geographically this continent was, and is, a masterpiece. With its ideal latitude and rich resources, the two-billion-acre expanse that became the United States was the promised land for active men.

The American continent was in a state of climax at the time of the first Indian intrusions ten millennia or more ago. Superlatives alone could describe the bewildering abundance of flora and fauna that enlivened its landscapes: the towering redwoods, the giant saguaro cacti, the teeming herds of buffalo, the beaver, and the grass were, of their kind, unsurpassed.

The most common trait of all primitive peoples is a reverence for the life-giving earth, and the native American shared this elemental ethic: the land was alive to his loving touch, and he, its son, was brother to all creatures."

— Stewart Udall, *The Quiet Crisis and the Next Generation*

Needle Creek forges through rocks and timber in the upper levels of Chicago Basin. It eventually finds its way into the Animas River, Weminuche Wilderness Area.

"We were climbing out of the Platte valley, going toward the high flatlands. Behind us the valley was lush with trees and irrigated fields. Ahead, where we were going, the hills rolled gently all the way to the horizon without a tree in sight."

— Hal Borland, *High, Wide and Lonesome*

In the darkness of predawn, sand bars remain black while the waters of the South Platte River reflect the arrival of morning, near the town of Sterling.

Imitating the sandy beaches and clear waters of the Caribbean Sea, the Green River is also a fine place for quiet contemplation, Dinosaur National Monument.

"A place is nothing in itself. It has no meaning, it can hardly be said to exist, except in terms of human perception, use, and response. The wealth and resources and usefulness of any region are only inert potential until man's hands and brain have gone to work; and natural beauty is nothing until it comes to the eye of the beholder. . . .

A look toward one's feet reveals a landscape as magnificent as those found upward — patterns sculpted by the waters of the Yampa River, Dinosaur National Monument.

. . . The natural world, actually, is the test by which each man proves
himself: I see, I feel, I love, I use, I alter, I appropriate, therefore I am. Or
the natural world is a screen onto which we project our own images;
without our images there, it is as blank as the cold screen of an empty
movie house."   — Wallace Stegner, *This Is Dinosaur*

This microcosm of nature implies that we do not need to look far to find integrity in the natural environment. Beauty in nature
is ubiquitous, North Colony Creek, Sangre de Cristo Wilderness Study Area.

" . . . it would be idiotic to preach conservation of . . . wilderness in
perpetuity, just to keep it safe from all human use. It is only for human use
that it has any meaning, or is worth preserving. But there is a vast difference
among uses. Some uses use things *up* and some last forever."

— Wallace Stegner, *This Is Dinosaur*

A look into this pool reveals the mountains of the Gore Range and a little bit more, Eagles Nest Wilderness Area, Gore Range.

Spring temperatures permit the Slate River to finally flow. Mount Crested Butte appears in the distance, Gunnison National Forest.

"We climbed out of the parks, up onto the rocky ridges where the spruce grew scarce, and then farther to the jumble of stones that had weathered from the great peaks above, and beyond that up the slope where all the vegetation was dwarfed, deformed, and weird, strange manifestation of its struggle for life. Here the air grew keener and cooler, and the light seemed to expand." — Zane Grey, *Tales of Lonely Trails*

Remains of a nighttime storm withdraw to reveal Lake Ann, flanked by the Three Apostles, Collegiate Peaks Wilderness Area.

"The creek was one pauseless torrent of white foam. All the beautiful amber spaces were gone. Not a breath did it take; it seemed like two miles of continuous waterfall. Tall fir-trees shaded it, . . . their shining darkness made the white of the foaming water all the whiter by contrast."
— Emily Faithfull, *Three Visits to America*

Frigid October temperatures create ice and rainbows on an upper stretch of the La Plata River, San Juan National Forest.

Rocky ridges bound the immense
cirque of Upper Ice Lake Basin,
San Juan National Forest.

Bless the Plants...

"After the council [man and the People of the Seed] all went to the plains and camped under the cedar and hemlock trees, building a great bower within which sacred symbols were made and prayers chanted. The ceremonies lasted a long time and included dances in which the boys and girls blessed the plants with caresses. Wherever they touched them, the plants burst into coloured flowers with beautiful tendrils. Then the Gods of the Four Seasons appeared from the east, and the food plants prospered. Man was now capable of living freely in the wide world."

Wildflowers of the Rockies, larkspur and Indian paintbrush among others, propagate in the wet and fertile soils around Kite Lake, Rio Grande National Forest, San Juan Mountains. Above: In the light of early morning, sunflowers adorn the dunes. Summer rain makes life possible in this otherwise arid environment, Great Sand Dunes National Monument.

"Groves of quakies, as the cowboys call the shimmering aspen trees, grow in many places throughout the Rockies. In Colorado they are perhaps the most characteristic vegetation of the mountains, giant rolling forests, their slim white boles, spotted with black, soaring to a canopy of leaves that the slightest wind sets to rustling and twinkling. In summer a sea-green luminosity filters through them; in autumn, after frost has burnished mile upon dazzling mile of them, it becomes an all-pervading golden haze." — David Lavender, *The Rockies*

Direct light on autumn's aspen makes brilliant color. Light diffused by a passing storm yields both color and detail, along Cucharas Pass, San Isabel National Forest.

In only a day, leaflets of lime green will emerge to make these aspen trees as colorful as their autumn counterparts, along Kebler Pass, Gunnison National Forest.

Something as common as a foot-square section of bark might provide incentive enough to go slowly along the trail — one of the benefits of a heavy backpack, Collegiate Peaks Wilderness Area.

Even without bark and life, our coniferous friends manifest their uncommon beauty. Nature's subtleties demand vigilance along the trail, Maroon Bells – Snowmass Wilderness Area.

"It was a surpassing sight! It is one of the few extended views I have seen which have also composition, beauty of grouping, and tenderness of significance and revelation. We could see long, shining, serrated spaces of the solid . . . peaks from whose summit one could look, if human vision were keen enough, to the Western and the Eastern Oceans. These lofty serrated lengths . . . cut against the uttermost horizon blue, like an alabaster wall rounding the very world. Seeming to join this wall, and almost in lines of concentric curves, were myriads and masses of lower mountains, more than the eye could count. To the very foot of the watch-tower ridge on which we stood, the peaks seemed crowded. We could look into the green valleys lying between them, and trace the brown thread of road winding up each valley. We sat under the shade of pines and firs. . . . Truly, labyrinths of interlacing hills can be marvellous. Much I question whether the earth holds anywhere a more delightful confusion than has been wrought out of these upheavals of the Rocky Mountains, and planted with firs and bluebells."

— Helen Hunt Jackson, *Bits of Travel at Home*

Mountain bluebells drink from the wetness of an alpine July. White Rock Mountain towers behind, Maroon Bells – Snowmass Wilderness Area.

"After the middle of September the aspens colored and blazed to the touch of frost, and the mountain slopes were exceedingly beautiful. Against a background of gray sage the gold and red and purple aspen groves showed too much like exquisite paintings to seem real."
— Zane Grey, *Tales of Lonely Trails*

Twin peaks of Mount Sopris, aspen and scrub oak enjoy the crisp air of a Colorado autumn day, White River National Forest.

"As we left ever farther behind us the wintry desolation of our high hunting grounds we rode into full spring. The green of the valley was a delight to the eye; bird songs sounded on every side, from the fields and from the trees and bushes beside the brooks . . . the air was sweet with the spring-time breath of many budding things."

— Theodore Roosevelt, *Outdoor Pastimes of an American Hunter*

Fed by waters from the Raggeds mountains, cottonwoods and aspen color the spring landscape, Gunnison National Forest.

Indian paintbrush garnish the
Continental Divide Trail,
Weminuche Wilderness Area.

In less than a square foot, lichen create art that might keep a painter busy for a week, high atop Trail Rider Pass, Maroon Bells – Snowmass Wilderness Area.

Using a similar palette, the artist broadens his scope to portray a garden of wildflowers below Mount Oso and Irving Peak, along Johnson Creek, Weminuche Wilderness Area.

"The hills were covered with buffalo grass or buffalo mixed with grama, and the draws, or valleys, were carpeted with bluestem. Here and there were clumps of yucca with their stiff, evergreen, bayonet leaves; and now and then we came to a hollow where sheep had grazed the grass away and cut it out with their sharp hoofs and sagebrush had taken over, sage and greasewood." — Hal Borland, *High, Wide and Lonesome*

Native grasses and grand cottonwood trees prepare for winter. The intermittent Arikaree River is usually dry, northeastern Colorado.

Alpine grasses begin to change color in September when the days are too short to keep the green, Flat Tops Wilderness Area.

"Despite the strenuous toil [of climbing] there were not many moments that I was not aware of the vastness of the gulf below, or the peaceful lakes, brown as amber, or the golden parks. And nearer at hand I found magenta-colored Indian paint brush, very exquisite and rare."

— Zane Grey, *Tales of Lonely Trails*

Not yet exposed to the light of a new day, Indian paintbrush wildflowers provide foreground to Huron Peak, Collegiate Peaks Wilderness Area.

On the high prairies of eastern Colorado, a wet summer allows plant life to perpetuate as it does in spring, along the Arikaree River, Yuma County.

"It was a picturesque spot. At this altitude it was still late winter and the snow lay in drifts, even in the creek bottom, while the stream itself was not yet clear from ice. The tents were pitched in a grove of leafless aspens and great spruces, beside the rushing, ice-rimmed brook."

— Theodore Roosevelt, *Outdoor Pastimes of an American Hunter*

Freshly fallen snow accentuates the maze of branches that gives winter's aspen trees their unique unfoliated character, White River National Forest.

Caught in torrential summer showers, a hiker's instinct is to run for cover. Yet patience and a good poncho can yield the visual joy of alpine wetness, West Maroon Pass, Maroon Bells – Snowmass Wilderness Area.

"Timbered country has spring subtleties, rising sap and first buds, florets on trees and bushes, half-hidden flowers among the rocks and leaf mold. But the plains are a vast simplicity at any season, their moods and changes swift, evident, and decisive. On that boundless open grassland neither spring nor any other season can hide or creep up slowly. Spring comes in a vast green wave rolling northward, a wave as evident as were the buffalo millions that once swept northward with new grass, as evident as the winter-hungry Indians that once swept northward with the buffalo. Spring on the plains has little more subtlety than a thunderstorm.

Winter ends, March drags its cold, muddy feet but finally passes, and there is spring, a rebirth that assaults all your senses. The surge of life at the grass roots penetrates your soles, creeps up through your bones, your marrow, and right into your heart. You see it, you feel it, you smell it, you taste it in every breath you breathe. You partake of spring. You are a part of it, even as you were a part of winter. Spring is all around you and in you, primal, simple as the plains themselves. Spring is, and you know it."

— Hal Borland, *High, Wide and Lonesome*

A sun almost gone still touches the high places — locoweed below the Pawnee Buttes, Pawnee National Grasslands, northeastern Colorado.

"Two miles from town we came to the end of the cottonwood lane. Ahead was the first range of sand hills. We turned. . . . We skirted the sand hills another mile to the east, then turned south again, and the hard road ended. The horses began to strain as the heavily laden wagon's wheels bit into the sand track."   — Hal Borland, *High, Wide and Lonesome*

Ancient sand dunes as old as the last ice age now foster native grasses in the sand hills of the South Platte River drainage, Weld County, eastern Colorado.

The dunes of the San Luis Valley are still young, yet they, too, support life as long as the rains come, Great Sand Dunes National Monument.

"It was a severe climb, — we did not know how severe, for our eyes were feasting on the wayside lovelinesses of green oak and juniper and golden asters, white daisies and purple vetches. From the bare and stony gulches we had left behind, to this fragrance and color, was a leap from a desert into a garden." — Helen Hunt Jackson, *Bits of Travel at Home*

Flowers of the non-native tamarisk plant lend color to the Dolores River Canyon. Great sandstone cliffs surround this western Colorado gorge.

"We crossed many little parks, bright and green, blooming with wild asters and Indian paint brush and golden daisies. The patches of red and purple were exceedingly beautiful. Everywhere we rode we were knee deep in flowers." — *Zane Grey, Tales of Lonely Trails*

Yellow paintbrush proliferate on top of 12,462-foot Buckskin Pass. In the distance looms Snowmass Peak, Maroon Bells — Snowmass Wilderness Area.

The Birth of Man...

"Sun Father cast his beams down upon the foam around the earth. He impregnated this Foam Mother and she [gave] birth to twins, the Preceder and the Follower, of the right hand and the left. Sun Father imparted to them some of his wisdom. He also gave them gifts: their mother the Foam Cloud, the rainbow, the thunderbolts and the fog-shield that makes clouds....Led...by the Preceder and the Follower, animals and men climbed the living ladder of growth into the Womb of Birth, where the light was like the dawn coming in the sky. The Twins began to instruct men, telling them that first of all they should seek the Sun, who would teach them the way of life of the upper world. Each of the tribes understood according to its ability. Their numbers increased until the Twins once again led them onward, this time into the outer world, the World of All-Spreading Light and Seeing."

Man uses aspen boles to make a fence as harmonious as nature could wish. It snakes its way toward the peaks of the Sneffels Range, San Juan Mountains.   Above: Winter snows consume all but the tops of this man-made boundary. Eventually nature will consume all of man's structures, Gunnison National Forest.

"You are rallying your own pride and your own strength, reaching back for some of the fortitude that was the mark of your own people. . . . It is a human impulse and a tribal necessity. When a man, or a people, forget where they came from and no longer look back with pride on their beginnings and confidence in their own blood and sinew and belief, that man or that people is doomed."   — Hal Borland, *High, Wide and Lonesome*

It's no wonder this dwelling has lasted for 50 years or more. Its construction was designed to withstand the violent thunderstorms of eastern Colorado, Washington County.

Seven thousand feet higher in elevation, a miner's cabin has perpetually withstood the weight of prodigious snows, Twin Lakes Basin, Weminuche Wilderness Area.

" . . . all through history man has been saying, 'I shall live here,' and finding the means to live where he chose. Either this earth is a remarkably habitable place or man is a favored creature. I would rather believe in the habitability of the earth. . . . The earth has its own pulse and rhythms, and the wise and fortunate man leans with the wind, sows with the season, and searches for water in valleys where water flows." —Hal Borland, *High, Wide and Lonesome*

A tumbleweed hides between rows of last year's corn crop. Late evening light colors all in its path, Baca County, southeastern Colorado.

The Great House in the Holly Group catches first light. At least 500 years old, these Anasazi Indian ruins are only several of more than 100,000 sites in the Four Corners area, Hovenweep National Monument.

"It is legitimate to hope that there may [be] left in Dinosaur the special kind of human mark, the special record of human passage, that distinguishes man from all other species. It is rare enough among men, impossible to any other form of life. *It is simply the deliberate and chosen refusal to make any marks at all.*" — Wallace Stegner, *This Is Dinosaur*

A sod roof is appropriate architecture for a sheepherder's shelter. The warmth of May will soon melt morning frost, Dinosaur National Monument.

"After such a storm, the world of the plains is a strange and magnificent place. It is as though all the earth-shaping forces have been at work on a vastly quickened scale of time. Hills, valleys, hollows and hummocks have all been reshaped to a new pattern. The wind has had its way, at last, the wind that is forever trying to level the hills and fill the valleys."
— Hal Borland, *High, Wide and Lonesome*

Great storms are common over the plains of southeastern Colorado. On their edges, the light is intense and saturates the land in yellow, Las Animas County.

"If we preserved as parks only those places that have no economic possibilities, we would have no parks. And in the decades to come, it will not be only the buffalo and the trumpeter swan who need sanctuaries. Our own species is going to need them too. It needs them now." — Wallace Stegner, *This Is Dinosaur*

The orange walls of Anasazi ruins radiate warmth after sunset. Pink hues reflect onto ancient stones and mortar, Cutthroat Castle, Hovenweep National Monument.

"Much mountain scenery is austere, violent, constricting. Then suddenly the land spreads out. . . . Streams coil quietly through meadows rather than dash headlong among boulders. Cattle and sheep graze as pastorally as in Iowa. There is no feeling of Iowa, however. Always on the horizon loom the snow-streaked peaks of another range. . . ."

— David Lavender, *The Rockies*

In mid-October, autumn begins to transform western Colorado. On the edge of Uncompahgre National Forest, scrub oak, aspen trees and 70-degree temperatures create a pleasant scene.

"One of the problems presented by the mythology of the Pueblo Indians is the richness and complexity of the material. The relationships between man and natural forces, the animal and the vegetable kingdoms, form the subject of a vast collection of myths which was combined and recombined in long ceremonies in which the myth was re-enacted by costumed actors.

The result was the integration of the people of the pueblo with their natural environment. There was no important event that was not related to man and the gods. Eagles were kept for a year by every family in the pueblo and then killed and sent to the gods to report on the world of men. Man depended on the blessing of the gods; the gods depended on the prayers and magical ceremonies of the people. The social system was naturally disrupted by the impact of the new and wider world of the white man; but there is evidence that the new ways have been assimilated without loss of all the ancient belief. A new relationship between man and his environment is evolving and it may be that the influence of American Indian philosophies and attitudes to life will become more important in the future."

— Cottie Burland, *Mythology of the Americas*

A large ceremonial kiva lies downhill from Lowry Pueblo Ruins. This large Anasazi site was home to many Native Americans at least 500 years ago, Montezuma County.

"We skied on in single file at a good pace. We plunged into thickets of spruce and fought our way through aspen. We glided easily and silently across open spaces. We heard and saw nothing. We did little talking."
— Private Harris Dusenbery, U.S. Army, 10th Mountain Division, "Ski the High Trail"

The solitude of winter is like that of no other season. A stroll on skis through the forest reacquaints a person with the meaning of peace, Routt National Forest.

"Father drew up the horses for a moment and just sat and looked....
I looked at him, and I looked again at the distance, and I felt a kind of
smile, inside myself, and a sense of awe that made me not want to say
a word. It was so big, so vast, so new, so wonderful."

— Hal Borland, *High, Wide and Lonesome*

Perhaps this section of land is resting from the strain of years of productivity. Nevertheless, its chromatic display is a visual
delight, Weld County, northeastern Colorado.

"That [the pueblos] don't crumble is a mystery. That these little squarish mud-heaps endure for centuries after centuries, while Greek marble tumbles asunder, and cathedrals totter, is the wonder. But then, the naked human hand with a bit of new soft mud is quicker than time, and defies the centuries." — D.H. Lawrence, *Mornings in Mexico*

Clinging to the side of a sheer sandstone cliff, Eagles Nest ruin was once home to the Anasazi. These unrestored dwellings are part of the Mesa Verde group, Ute Mountain Indian Reservation, Montezuma County.

Lowry Pueblo Ruins receive pink light from sunrise. In the distance slumbers sacred Sleeping Ute Mountain at 9,977 feet, southwestern Colorado.

Lodgepole lupine wildflowers create
a garden of color beside an
old homestead, Williams Fork
Mountains.

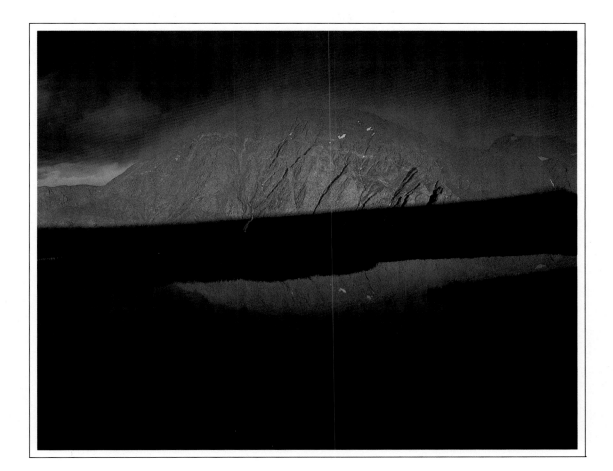

The Navel of the Earth...

"The emergence of man was completed and the social order established. Men next had to learn how to live in the world under the sun. But the world was new and tormented, with vast swamps inhabited by monsters, desolate plains of broken rock, and earthquakes. It was necessary for men to seek more secure dwelling places. On the journey they were led by the beloved Twins who told them to rest awhile at a camp called the Place of Uprising which faced the sunrise. At this camp they were instructed to travel towards the east, where Father Sun arose, until they came to the Navel of the Earth. Only there would they find peace and stability."

On the plains in spring it is not uncommon for fierce storms to appear at the crack of dawn. Blackness consumes the landscape, but not before the sun does its work, Pawnee National Grasslands.   Above: Eagles Nest Peak, at 13,397 feet, receives the light of a sun freed from the cover of thick, wet clouds. What started as an evening in the tent became a celebration of nature, Eagles Nest Wilderness Area, Gore Range.

"Each generation has its own rendezvous with the land, for despite our fee titles and claims of ownership, we are all brief tenants on this planet. By choice, or by default, we will carve out a land legacy for our heirs. We can misuse the land and diminish the usefulness of resources, or we can create a world in which physical affluence and affluence of the spirit go hand in hand." — Stewart Udall, *The Quiet Crisis and the Next Generation*

Moving with alacrity, spring clouds paint a motion picture's worth of scenes on aspen trees in Uncompahgre National Forest. This was just one, near Telluride.

Similarly, clouds receding from a fast-moving storm deposit sunlight and fresh snow in fortuitous patterns of visual joy, Routt National Forest.

The descending sun sends its magnetic rays across the plains. Particulates in the air cast orange light over all things in their path, Arikaree River, Yuma County.

Pilot Knob Peak catches first light. The rays of the sun will slowly work their way down into the valley — from Lower Ice Lake Basin, San Juan Mountains.

"It is ironical that today the conservation movement finds itself turning back to ancient Indian land ideas, to the Indian understanding that we are not outside of nature, but of it. From this wisdom we can learn how to conserve the best parts of our continent."
— Stewart Udall, *The Quiet Crisis and the Next Generation*

Warmth from the sun makes snow on the dunes short-lived. Until it is gone, rejoice in the pairing of snow and sand, Great Sand Dunes National Monument.

"The peace of nature and of the innocent creatures of God seems to be secure and deep, only so long as the presence of man and his restless and unquiet spirit are not there to trouble its sanctity."
— Thomas De Quincey, *Confessions of an English Opium-Eater*

Brutal winds plaster snow to lodgepole pine trees. Here, too, the sun will soon wreck this marvelous moment that nature briefly allows, Arapaho National Forest.

"Between Pueblo and Bent's fort, southward, in a clear afternoon sun-spell I catch exceptionally good glimpses of the Spanish peaks. We are in southeastern Colorado — pass immense herds of cattle as our first-class locomotive rushes us along — two or three times crossing the Arkansas, which we follow many miles, and of which river I get fine views, sometimes for quite a distance, its stony, upright, not very high, palisade banks, and then its muddy flats. We pass Fort Lyon — lots of adobie houses — limitless pasturage, appropriately fleck'd with those herds of cattle — in due time the declining sun in the west — a sky of limpid pearl over all — and so evening on the great plains. A calm, pensive, boundless landscape— the perpendicular rocks of the north Arkansas, hued in twilight — a thin line of violet on the southwestern horizon — the palpable coolness and slight aroma — a belated cow-boy with some unruly member of his herd — an emigrant wagon toiling yet a little further, the horses slow and tired . . . and around all the indescribable *chiaroscuro* and sentiment, (profounder than anything at sea,) athwart these endless wilds."

— Walt Whitman, *Prose Works* . . .

In less than an hour, an autumn snowstorm deposits its white dust and moves along. West Spanish Peak reappears, Spanish Peaks Wilderness Study Area.

"We lose a great deal, I think, when we lose this sense and feeling for the sun. When all has been said, the adventure of the sun is the great natural drama by which we live, and not to have joy in it and awe of it, not to share in it, is to close a dull door on Nature's sustaining and poetic spirit." — Henry Beston, *The Outermost House*

Sunsets are an evolution of events involving the sun and the atmosphere. As in theater, the denouement is often the most exciting part of the drama, Collegiate Peaks Wilderness Area.

After a night of constant rain the skies begin to clear, but not before nature puts on its last act. My seat is Frigid Air Pass and the stage is the Maroon Bells – Snowmass Wilderness Area.

"The sunset that evening was a worthy pendant to the sunrise . . . the last glorious rays of the departing sun lighted up the peaks and snowy summits of the mountains with a brilliancy of color no artist would dare, even were it possible, to represent on canvas; and then, as there is no twilight here, darkness quickly ensued. . . . "

— Emily Faithfull, *Three Visits to America*

The setting sun coats white snow with red. Barren aspen cast shadows across the spilled paint, Routt National Forest, near Buffalo Pass.

" . . . there is an everchanging panorama of snow-crowned mountains,
deep gorges, forest-covered slopes, and a remembrance for a lifetime.
Even those to whom the Alps, the Andes, and the Himalayas are familiar,
will appreciate the glimpses of glory to be obtained as they stand on the
brink of . . . the Rocky Mountains." — Emily Faithfull, *Three Visits to America*

Cathedral Peak, at 13,943 feet, receives first light on a 15-below-zero February morning. At 12,000 feet the winter landscape
is consumed by white, White River National Forest.

"Commonly we stride through the out-of-doors too swiftly to see more than the most obvious and prominent things. For observing nature, the best pace is a snail's pace." — Edwin Way Teale, *Circle of the Seasons*

Light from the setting sun breaks through the moistness of an autumn storm. Its rays highlight aspen trees and scrub oak below mountains of the West Elk Wilderness Area, Kebler Pass.

Afternoon showers approach, but not before the sun paints its warmth on the rocky landscape of Silver Mesa, Weminuche Wilderness Area, San Juan Mountains.

"That the sky is brighter than the earth means little unless the earth itself is appreciated and enjoyed. Its beauty loved gives the right to aspire to the radiance of the sunrise and the stars." — Helen Keller, *My Religion*

Silhouettes and their reflections create shapes in the alpine world. A rising sun will soon erase the scene, along the Continental Divide Trail, Weminuche Wilderness Area.

Cliffs 2,000 feet high are not uncommon along the edges of the Yampa River. Meanders continue to erode soft sandstone walls, Dinosaur National Monument.

"The sky above this young fairyland is in every particular becoming to the landscapes it mantles; usually, pale, tender blue, with pearl clouds hovering in calm, fleecy, filmy masses, combed out on the luminous edges, but never garish-colored. Morning and evening are in orange, purple, and red, and at noon in summer the whole bland atmosphere palpitates with an intense subdued passion of light, in which the tranquil sheets of water shimmer and spangle, and the evergreens of the islands dip their spires with inimitable grace and repose."

— *The Unpublished Journals of John Muir*

The remains of an afternoon shower cling to mountains of the Collegiate Peaks Wilderness Area. A tarn at almost 13,000 feet mirrors the event, Missouri Creek basin.

"For the man sound in body and serene of mind there is no such thing as bad weather; every sky has its beauty, and storms which whip the blood do but make it pulse more vigorously."
— George Gissing, *The Private Papers of Henry Ryecroft*

Blizzard conditions cut visibility to less than 20 feet. Windblown conifers survive on a rocky ledge, White River National Forest.

"The woods arise in shaggy majesty, every light giving tints of exquisite softness to all the wilderness. Trees ancient-looking abound in damp gullies and on stream-banks, forming the forest primeval. . . . Here are true Gothic temples with tree-shafts pointed and aspiring."
— *The Unpublished Journals of John Muir*

Last night's rain departs the scene as the ascending sun warms the forest near the tiny town of Tincup, Gunnison National Forest.

"Talk as you like, a typical Rocky Mountain cañon, or a limitless sea-like stretch of the great Kansas or Colorado plains, under favoring circumstances, tallies, perhaps expresses, certainly awakes, those grandest and subtlest element-emotions in the human soul, that all the marble temples and sculptures . . . all paintings, poems, reminiscences, or even music, probably never can." — Walt Whitman, *Prose Works . . .*

August skies highlight peaks of the Gore Range. Water in one of the Upper Slate Lakes scurries about in cool morning winds, Eagles Nest Wilderness Area.

East Pawnee Butte receives light from the sun just as it breaks the horizon. Wildflowers await their own chance to bask, Pawnee National Grasslands.

"But it is not in the deeps of the woods that people are soothed into perfect rest, nor in mountain valleys, however beautifully bounded by lofty walls. One feels submerged and ever seeks the free expanse. Nor yet on lofty summits, islands of the sky, but on the tranquil uplands where exhilarating air. . .

In sub-zero temperatures a decrepit old pine and winter's rabbitbrush absorb rays of the descending sun, Great Sand Dunes National Monument.

. . . and a free far outlook are combined with the loveliest of the flora. In that zone below the ice and snow and above the darkling woods, where the sunshine sleeps on alpine gardens and the young rivers flow rejoicing from the glacial caves . . . perfect quietude is there, and freedom from every curable care." *— The Unpublished Journals of John Muir*

The end of a storm is like the last five pages of a good mystery. The kind of ending it will have is difficult to predict, but it is usually exciting, Sangre de Cristo Wilderness Study Area.

The end of the storm, Eagles Nest
Wilderness Area.

Acknowledgements

With the burden of much heavy camera gear, it is often difficult to go as fast and far as curiosity demands. The work of the past few years would have been much less productive were it not for the help of my "sherpas," loyal lovers of the wilderness who helped me carry my gear, prepare dinners and shepherd the llamas. This assistance allowed me to devote most of my time to the tasks of scouting and photographing, instead of worrying about surviving in what can be a hostile environment. I was, therefore, more creative and perceptive thanks to the help of these friends of mine and nature: Bill Gardner, Brian Litz, Paul Gallaher, Barry Johnson and Dennis Johns. I am also grateful to Tom Till, one of our country's great nature photographers, for showing me parts of western Colorado, and to Sidney Macy and Kim Youngblood, of the Colorado Nature Conservancy, for exposing me to parts of eastern Colorado. Finally, thanks to Bob Reed and his associates at Reed Photo Art for developing the original transparencies with such great care.

Technical Information

The spring, summer and autumn images in this book were made with a Linhof Technika 4x5 view camera. The winter scenes were made with a Pentax 6x7 single lens reflex camera. Lens focal lengths used with the Linhof ranged from 75mm to 500mm, and from 45mm to 200mm with the Pentax. I used a Pentax digital 1-degree spot meter to calculate exposures by using reflected light from the landscape and a gray card. In cloudy light I employed 81A and 81B warming filters. Kodak Ektachrome and Fuji Fujichrome films were used to make the original transparencies.

— J.F.

Now let us reflect upon the worth of our natural environment, Eagles Nest Wilderness Area, Gore Range.